I0934427

DAY OF THE DEAD

Joanna Ponto and Carol Gnojewski

Enslow Publishing
101 W. 23rd Street
Suite 240
New York, NY 10011
USA
enslow.com

Published in 2017 by Enslow Publishing, LLC.
101 W. 23rd Street, Suite 240, New York, NY 10011

Library of Congress Cataloging-in-Publication Data
Names: Ponto, Joanna, author. | Gnojewski, Carol, author.
Title: Day of the Dead / Joanna Ponto and Carol Gnojewski.
Description: New York, NY : Enslow Publishing, [2017] | Series: The story of our holidays | Includes
bibliographical references and index. | Audience: Grades 4-6.
Identifiers: LCCN 2016001031| ISBN 9780766076440 (library bound) | ISBN 9780766076426 (pbk.) |
ISBN 9780766076433 (6-pack)
Subjects: LCSH: All Souls' Day--Mexico--Juvenile literature. | Mexico--Social
  life and customs--Juvenile literature.
Classification: LCC GT4995.A4 P665 2016 | DDC 394.266--dc23
LC record available at http://lccn.loc.gov/2016001031

Printed in the United States of America

To Our Readers: We have done our best to make sure all website addresses in this book were active and appropriate when we went to press. However, the author and the publisher have no control over and assume no liability for the material available on those websites or on any websites they may link to. Any comments or suggestions can be sent by e-mail to customerservice@enslow.com.

Portions of this book originally appeared in the book *Day of the Dead: A Latino Celebration of Family and Life* by Carol Gnojewski.

Photo Credits: Cover, p. 1 Tino Soraino/National Geographic/Getty Images; p. 4 Kobby Dagan/ Shutterstock.com; p. 6 JAIME REINA/AFP/Getty Images; p. 7 CRIS BOURONCLE/AFP/Getty Images; p. 9 underworld/Shutterstock.com; p. 11 De Agostini/G. Dagli Orti/Getty Images; p. 14 Dorling Kindersley/Getty Images; p. 15 Jan Sochor/Latincontent/Getty Images; p. 17 Inakiherrasti/Wikimedia Commons/Ofrenda Dolores Olmedo.15.JPG/CC BY-SA 4.0; p. 19 James Southers/Alamy Stock Photo; p. 22 C M Christopher Wong/Moment/Getty Images; pp. 23, 27 AGCuesta/Shutterstock.com; p. 25 US Marine Corps./Wikimedia Commons/USMC-090414-M-6796M-150.jpg/public domain; p. 29 Cathy Tardosky.

Contents

Children dressed in Day of the Dead costumes participate in a carnival.

Chapter 1

Party in the Cemetery

On November 1, people in villages throughout Mexico prepare for a big picnic. Everyone is in a festive mood. Church bells toll. Fireworks explode. They announce the arrival of special guests. The spirits of the dead are coming!

A Festive Environment

In the afternoon, families carry *canastas*, or baskets, filled with food and supplies to the cemetery. They clean and weed around the headstones of relatives. Once the graves are tidied, families sit together and eat.

It is crowded in the cemetery. The whole town is there. Kids play games with friends. Musicians called *mariachis* stroll among the graves. They sing popular songs. People sell balloons and flowers outside the cemetery.

People clean the tombstones of their family members on Day of the Dead.

As night falls, candles are placed on the graves. There is one candle for each dead family member. One by one the candles are lit. The names of the dead are said aloud. Shadows from the flickering candles dance from face to face and tomb to tomb.

All night long, the picnic continues. Families stay awake and keep dead relatives company. They gossip and share family stories. They remember the good times they had with those who have died.

A Day of Healing

In the United States, death is not often openly talked about. When a person dies, there are services held before the burial. Cemeteries are sometimes located far away from city centers. After dark, they are not meeting places for the living. To people in the United States, spending the night in a cemetery may sound like a scene in a scary movie.

Tomb Tables

Many Mexican cemeteries have raised stone tombs. Families use them as tables when they gather around them during Day of the Dead. Gifts for the dead are spread on top of the tombs. These gifts might be flowers, candles, candies, and food.

It is not thought of as scary in Mexico. Picnicking with dead relatives is one way that many Mexicans celebrate a sacred holiday called Los Días de los Muertos. In Spanish this means the Days of the Dead. Sometimes Days of the Dead is called Day of the Dead.

The Day of the Dead is celebrated from October 31 to November 2. This is an important holiday in Mexico because it centers on the family and the stages of life and death. Since ancient times, Mexicans have set aside these days for spiritual and family healing.

After the headstones have been cleaned and tidied, families eat a big meal at the gravesite.

Chapter 2

Aztec Views on Life and Death

The ancient people known as the Aztecs lived on the land that is now the country of Mexico from the fourteenth to sixteenth centuries. The Aztecs saw that the growing season came and went in a regular cycle. Stars also changed positions in a set way that they could remember and record.

Their interest in the sky led the Aztecs to make a solar calendar, sometimes called the Sun Calendar. It is a large disk made of green volcanic stone. The disk shows time in a series of circles with the sun in the center. There are circles within circles. This meant that time and life repeated itself.

Making Room for Others

Tonatiuh, the sun, was one of many *teotl*, or gods, that the Aztecs worshipped. They believed it was the giver of life. Tonatiuh died each evening to make night possible. To the Aztecs, this meant people died to make room for others.

Aztecs thought of human life as a cycle that did not end in death. Though a person's body was buried in the ground, his or her spirit lived on. It mattered how someone died and not how he or she lived. Dead warriors became hummingbirds and flew to the sun. Babies went to a land where milk dripped from trees. There was even a special place for people who drowned or were struck by lightning.

The Aztec calendar features a sun at its center. The Aztecs worshipped the sun.

Most souls walked on an endless road called Mictlán. This was the underworld. Clothing, tools, and pots were buried with people for use on their journey. The Lord of Death, Mictlantecuhtli, guarded their bones. The Aztecs feared him. However, they did not think him evil. He was both greedy and generous. He had the power to create life or to take it away.

Rebirth

The Aztecs thought that when night ended, the sun was reborn. The Aztecs believed that the dead would rise again, too. They believed that dead bodies waited for rebirth like seeds in the soil. Festivals for the dead were held throughout the year in the ninth and tenth months of the Sun Calendar. These months fell in late summer. Wealthy families shared food with poorer families. They

The Aztec Calendar Stone

The Aztec calendar stone, also known as the Sun Stone, was carved from a hard rock called basalt in the sixteenth century. It stands 12 feet (3.6 meters) wide and weighs almost 25 tons (22 metric tons). Carved figures on the stone stand for months and years.

This Aztec funerary urn depicts Mictlantecuhtli, the Lord of Death. He was a very powerful god to the Aztecs.

also invited the dead spirits to visit them.

Since these souls had passed on to a new level of the universe, the Aztecs treated them like gods. Strong incense called *copal* was burned. Copal is made from tree sap. The Aztecs imagined that its smoke reached Mictlán. It led the dead from Mictlán to the homes of family and friends. Shrines for the dead were decorated with bark paper called *amatl*. Newly harvested fruits, vegetables, and flowers were heaped upon them.

Chapter 3

The Spanish Arrive in Mexico

In 1521, Spanish soldiers conquered Mexico. They overthrew the Aztec Empire and took over the Aztec cities. Mexico became a Spanish colony. Many Aztecs were enslaved. The soldiers wanted to get rid of the Aztec way of life. First, they tore down the Aztec temples and built Spanish churches on the same ground. Then they brought in Spanish priests called missionaries.

Catholic Beliefs

Missionaries taught the Aztecs about the Catholic religion. They hoped it would replace their ancient beliefs. The Catholic Church was very powerful at this time. The Spanish missionaries worshipped one God instead of many. They believed in an afterlife for the soul. Souls were judged at death for their deeds in life.

The missionaries tried to teach Christianity to the Aztecs. They taught them about the lives of Catholic saints and martyrs. Some people with a special relationship to God became saints. Martyrs had been killed for their Christian beliefs. The missionaries compared saints and martyrs to the Aztec gods.

Cortés the Conqueror

Hernán Cortés was a Spanish explorer. Cortés was born in Spain around 1485. He helped conquer the island of Cuba in 1511. From Cuba, he sailed to Mexico in 1519. Cortés heard about the Aztec Empire. By 1521, Cortés had conquered the Aztecs and controlled most of central Mexico. Hernán Cortés died in 1547 near Seville, Spain.

All Souls' Day

Like the Aztecs, Spanish missionaries honored the dead on a special days, such as All Saints' Day, which is November 1. Showing respect to the saints on this day was thought to bring protection to the living. November 2 is All Souls' Day. This festival began in Europe

The Europeans converted the Aztecs to Christianity. They were baptized and taught to worship the Christians' God.

in the ninth century. On this day, the people of Spain asked God to send the souls of their loved ones to heaven. They placed food and candles on family graves in churches and cemeteries. This custom closely matched the Aztec offering.

To celebrate Day of the Dead, families make altars to their dead loved ones.

Mexico became independent from Spain in 1821. For three hundred years, Aztecs and other Mexican people tried to keep their beliefs separate from the Spanish. Yet over time, Spanish and Aztec traditions blended together. Now each region of Mexico has different ways of celebrating the Days of the Dead. One common practice is the making of an *ofrenda*, or altar. Ofrendas give families the chance to offer their love and to remember those who have died.

Chapter 4

Day of the Dead Altars

In Aztec temples and Spanish churches, people placed gifts for the gods and spirits on altars. Today, altars are special areas set up in people's homes.

Altars can be found in many Spanish and Mexican homes. Families spend quiet moments around them singing and praying. Some fill an entire room. Others take up a corner of one. Home altars honor saints and family members. Photos, candles, religious statues, and prayer beads are often placed upon them.

Putting Together an Ofrenda

Everyone in the family gets involved in making an ofrenda for the Days of the Dead. First, they share memories about their dead relatives. What did they enjoy when they were alive? How did they dress? Which were their favorite movies, books, or foods? Things they liked or that belonged to them are placed on the altar. For example, if a dead relative played guitar, a real or a toy guitar might be added.

An ofrenda is meant to honor the life of the departed. It may include photos, trinkets, and other symbols.

For the Dead

Here are some examples of offerings that people leave for the dead:

- *Papel picado*—a cut paper mat
- Candles—one for each dead family member
- Skulls made of wood or sugar
- Soap and a small towel for washing
- Water for drinking
- Salt—a symbol of life
- Incense
- Bread
- Spicy foods
- Flowers
- Chocolate

The ofrenda creates a space for the dead in a family's daily life. Dead relatives seem closer when their stories are retold. By making an ofrenda, families show each other how much dead loved ones still mean to them. Children learn their family history.

Some families believe that the spirits themselves visit their homes during this time. In the state of Morelos, Mexico, the altar is set up in a bedroom with chairs or a bed for the dead to rest on. The living then sleep on the front porch. This is not done out of fear. They want to make the dead comfortable.

Outside the Home

Ofrendas may be set up outside the home. Some are placed near graves or at the place where a person died. In central Mexico, people build them on boats and barges. They float them down the canals.

Museums and galleries often honor famous people with fancy ofrendas. Churches and community centers may make simple ofrendas for people who are often forgotten, such as orphans or prisoners. In the *zócalos*, or town squares in cities, artists and activists create public altars that can be seen by everyone. These altars often draw attention to people who died from hunger, disease, or unsafe working conditions.

In some parts of Mexico, ofrendas are built on boats and floated out into the water.

Chapter 5

Offerings to the Dead

Ofrendas almost always include foods and flowers. This traces back to the altars of the Aztecs, which were heaped with symbols of the harvest.

Marigolds

Marigolds, or *cempasuchitl*, are known as the flower of the dead. They are yellow-orange and smell earthy. Their bright color reminded the Aztecs of the sun. During the Days of the Dead, marigold flowers are arranged in vases, planted near graves, and strung onto cane wreaths or arches. The arches form a door for the dead to enter.

Flower petals also are scattered over graves. Families make a path of seeds and petals from the cemetery to their homes. They expect the dead to follow this path. It is believed that marigolds are bright enough for the dead to see after living in so much darkness.

Cempasuchitl

Mexico is famous for its flowers. Marigolds, or cempasuchitl, bloom there in the fall. *Cempasuchitl* means "flower of twenty petals."

Food Offerings

Food is present on most altars, too. Markets are loaded with fresh fruits and vegetables. Families fill their baskets with oranges, chilis, tomatoes, and sugarcane. Some of these are added directly to the altar. Others are made into rich and spicy dishes.

Mole is a thick slow-cooked sauce served with stewed turkey or chicken. Cocoa beans are hand-ground into powder and added to the sauce. The Aztecs were the first to use chocolate in their cooking. Mexicans are well-known for their hot chocolate, which is often spiced with chili or cinnamon. Try the Mexican hot chocolate recipe on page 27.

No offering is complete without *pan de muertos*, or bread of the dead. This sweet egg bread is flavored with cinnamon or anise, which tastes like black licorice. The bread is then glazed with honey or sprinkled with sugar. Sometimes the loaves are shaped like people or animals. This mimics the Aztec custom of placing corn dough figures on temple altars. A popular pan de muertos shape is that of a skull. In some bakeries, dough is made into bones and baked atop round loaves.

Marigolds and lights are used to decorate graves. The bright flowers are meant to guide the dead from darkness.

To welcome the dead, people leave offerings of pan de muertos.

Offerings of food make dead guests feel welcome in the homes of the living. The dead cannot really eat the food. They are thought to inhale its wonderful smell. When the dead leave, families make a meal of what is left on the altar.

Any act of eating is a form of sacrifice. All food comes from the dead bodies of plants and animals. Many people go from house to house and exchange food. As they do, they say to each other, "This is a gift from my dead relative." Legends warn that if you are not generous with your offering then you will have bad luck in the next year.

Chapter 6

Day of the Dead Skulls

During the Day of the Dead holiday, skulls and skeletons can be seen everywhere. They are a symbol of the Day of the Dead much like they are a symbol of Halloween in the United States.

Skeletons and Skulls

Stores carry skeleton puppets, cutouts, and figurines. Skeleton toys wear clothes and are posed on everything from bicycles to barber chairs. These toys are based on the engravings of an artist named José Guadalupe Posada. Posada lived and worked in Mexico during the late 1800s. His art was printed in newspapers and pamphlets. Posada's skeletons are silly and not spooky. They remind us that skeletons support our bodies.

Skulls and skeletons are symbols of the Day of the Dead. Shops sell all kinds of decorated skulls.

Underneath our clothes and skin, we are all skeletons, too.

Bakeries paint skeletons on their windows to advertise their holiday breads and cakes. They sell skull-shaped treats made of chocolate or sugar. Sugar skulls are given as gifts. Families place them on the graves of young children. These unusual candies are covered with swirling patterns and shiny foil strips. Slips of paper with names written on them are attached to the candy forehead. You can eat a skull with your name on it or with the name of a friend.

Other Ways of Celebrating

In some neighborhoods, children go skulling. They travel from house to house carrying real or plastic pumpkins. At each door, they stop to recite funny verses called *calaveras*. The poems poke fun at famous people, such as actors, athletes, and politicians. Adults then hand out coins, nuts, or candy. This custom is called *calavereando*.

Hispanic communities throughout the United States celebrate the Days of the Dead. Their fiestas, or parties, may have candle-lighting ceremonies, altar making, and sugar skull decorating. For many Mexican Americans, this is a way of passing on their traditions to family and friends. It is a good way to remember history and to bring it back to life—even if only for a day or two.

Sugar Skulls

Stacked on candy store shelves, rows of sugar skulls look like *tzompantli*. These were racks that Aztecs used to dry out human skulls. Holes were drilled through the skulls so that they could be strung side by side on wooden rods like beads.

Champurrado (Mexican Hot Chocolate)*

Ingredients:

4 cups (950 mL) milk
2 cups (475 mL) water
1 stick cinnamon
3 ½ oz (100 g) bittersweet
  baking chocolate, or
  tablet Mexican chocolate
6 oz (170 g) whole cane
  sugar, or piloncillo
½ cup (60 g) corn flour

Directions:

1. Pour the milk into a saucepan and add the sugar, cinnamon, and chocolate.

2. Simmer the milk on low, stirring occasionally with a whisk, until the chocolate and sugar have melted.

3. In a separate bowl, whisk the water and corn flour together until the corn flour is completely dissolved. Make sure there are no lumps left!

4. Stir the water and corn flour mixture into the milk and chocolate in the saucepan.

5. Continue to simmer the liquid on low, stirring occasionally with the whisk, for 8–10 minutes. When the champurrado is done it will be thick like gravy.

6. Remove the cinnamon stick and serve in mugs.

* Adult supervision required.

Day of the Dead Craft*

Skeletons are displayed everywhere in honor of the Day of the Dead. Try making one yourself!

Here are the supplies you will need:

white pipe cleaners
foam packing peanuts
permanent black marker
string (optional)

Directions:

1. Join two pipe cleaners at the center by twisting them together three times. This will make an X shape. The lower half of the X will form the legs of the skeleton and the upper half will be the body.

2. Form a small loop at the bottom of each leg and twist to make feet.

3. Twist the top halves together so they make one strand.

4. Bend the top half and twist together so the body is thicker than the legs.

5. Form one small loop on each end of a third pipe cleaner. These are the skeleton's hands.

6. Place the third pipe cleaner perpendicular to the body near the center and twist to attach.

Bendable Skeleton

7. Draw a skeletal face onto a packing peanut using a permanent black marker.

8. Attach the head by inserting it onto the top of the body. Use a gentle twisting motion or the peanut may break.

9. Bend the arms and legs into interesting poses.

If you wish, tie a length of string under the packing peanut skull and hang your skeleton near a Day of the Dead display. You can also use the hand loops for hanging.

*Safety note: Be sure to ask for help from an adult, if needed, to complete this project.

29

Glossary

altar—A platform or table used as a center of worship.

canal—A long, narrow passageway filled with water on which people use boats to get from place to place.

Christianity— A religion based on the teachings of Jesus Christ.

missionary—A person sent to spread a religious faith.

offering—A gift given to the dead.

ofrenda—A collection of objects placed on an altar to the dead.

tomb—A large vault for burying the dead.

tradition—The handing down of information or customs from parents to their children.

underworld—The place of departed souls.

Learn More

Books

Jones, Karl, and Steve Simpson. *Day of the Dead Activity Book.* New York, NY: Price Stern Sloan, 2013.

Jones, Theodore. *Celebrating Day of the Dead.* New York, NY: Gareth Stevens Publishing, 2016.

McGee, Randel. *Celebrate Day of the Dead With Paper Crafts.* Berkeley Heights, NJ: Enslow Elementary, 2015.

Murray, Julie. *Day of the Dead.* Edina, MN: ABDO Publishing Company, 2014.

Websites

Enchanted Learning: Day of the Dead Mexican Crafts and Activities

www.enchantedlearning.com/crafts/dayofthedead/
   Make fun crafts to celebrate Day of the Dead.

DLTK: Day of the Dead Crafts and Activities for Kids

dltk-kids.com/world/mexico/day-of-the-dead.htm
   Find crafts, coloring pages, and puzzles on this fun site.

Enchanted Learning: Mexico

enchantedlearning.com/school/mexico
   Click on the pictures to find out more about Mexico from this Zoom School website.

Index